DOING THE SAME IN ENGLISH

First published in 2008 by
The Dedalus Press
13 Moyclare Road
Baldoyle
Dublin 13
Ireland

www.dedaluspress.com

Copyright © Maurice Scully, 2008

ISBN 978 1 906614 00 3

All rights reserved.
No part of this publication may be reproduced in any form or by
any means without the prior permission of the publisher.

Dedalus Press titles are represented in North America
by Syracuse University Press, Inc., 621 Skytop Road,
Suite 110, Syracuse, New York 13244, and in the UK by
Central Books, 99 Wallis Road, London E9 5LN

Cover painting
Rocks (2008, oil on linen, 59 x 20 mm)
by Leda Scully

The Dedalus Press receives financial assistance from
An Chomhairle Ealaíon / The Arts Council, Ireland

DOING THE SAME IN ENGLISH

A Sampler of Work 1987—2008

Maurice Scully

DEDALUS PRESS
DUBLIN, IRELAND

Also by Maurice Scully:

Poetry

Love Poems & Others (Raven Arts Press, 1981)
5 Freedoms of Movement (Galloping Dog Press, 1987)
Prior (Staple Diet, 1991; tel-let, 1992)
Certain Pages (Form Books, 1992)
Over and Through (Poetical Histories, 1992)
The Basic Colours (Pig Press, 1994)
Priority (Writers Forum, 1995)
Prelude, Interlude and *Postlude* (all Wild Honey Press, 1997)
Steps (Reality Street Editions, 1998)
Etruscan Reader IV
    (with Bob Cobbing & Carlyle Reedy: Etruscan Books, 1996, 1999)
5 Freedoms of Movement (revised edition, Etruscan Books, 2001)
Tree with Eggs (hardPressed poetry, 2004)
Livelihood (Wild Honey Press, 2004)
Numbers (Coracle Press, 2006)
Sonata (Reality Street Editions, 2006)
Tig (Shearsman Books, 2006)

CD

Mouthpuller (Wild Honey Press/Coelacanth Press, 2000)

Children's

What Is The Cat Looking At? (Faber, 1995)

For my kids—Leda, Louis, Hazel and Paul

ACKNOWLEDGEMENTS

Cover painting: *Rocks*, (2008, oil on linen, 59 x 20 mm) by Leda Scully.
Priority frontispiece by Leda Scully, then aged 8.
Title page photo for Two Caterpillars by Kenneth Josephson.
All other graphics by the author.
Author photo by Hazel Scully, 2008.

Contents

THINGS THAT HAPPEN (1981—2006)

from *5 Freedoms of Movement* (1987)
Two Caterpillars / 11

from *Priority* (1995)
In the Music / 27
Maturity / 28
Sound / 29
Rain / 30
Sonnet / 32
Rain / 33
Sonnet / 34
In the Music / 35
Point / 36
Sound / 37
Liking the Big Wheelbarrow / 38
A Personal Note / 39
And Through / 40

from *Steps* (1998)
In the Music / 45
Marching Song / 46
In Praise of Painting Doors / 48
Fire / 50
Permission / 51
Responsibility / 53
Rain / 54
Steps / 55
Four Corners / 57
Fire / 59

from *Adherence* (2004)
A, B, C / 67
Cohering / 79

from *Postlude* (1997)
The tree beside ... / 101

from *Sonata* (2006)
A Song (& A Dance) / 107
Song / 115
Sonnet / 117
black. a dot. a dark dot moving ... / 120

from *Tig* (2006)
[Blessing the Animals] / 127
[Picking Persimmon] / 130
[A Place to Stay] / 135
Coda / 138

NEW BOOKS (2004—2008)

from *Humming*
Sonnet Song / 145
Ballad / 149
Sing ... / 154
Song / 156

from *Several Dances*
On a Light Ground: Eye Dance / 161
On a Dark Ground: Work Dance / 163
Lyric: Bal/ancing / 166
Mountain Railway: Gavotte / 168
[Hungarian] Folk Dance: Artist's Studio / 169
To Balance / 172
Rain Dance / 174
Locket / 177
Neighbouring Doors (Ceremonial Dance) / 178

from *Work*
Geometric / 183
Setting / 189
Long Block / 191

NOTES / 200

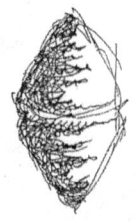

⬙ : *legal, decision, trial* or *peace*

TWO CATERPILLARS

*There once were two young caterpillars, Fat
Caterpillar and Fatter Caterpillar, that lived
on a windowsill under a tree. The windowsill
was white and the caterpillars were white and
green and they ate and ate and slept and slept
quite happily on the white windowsill under
the tree.*

*One day a bankman came to the tree with his
money and sat under it balancing a book. But
he soon fell asleep and began to dream. And
in his dream he saw a bankman falling asleep
under a tree with his money and a book and
beginning to dream of a man dreaming he was
making money out of a book (in which he featured
quite prominently) under a tree beside a window-
sill upon which were two young caterpillars,
laughing, white and green, Fat Caterpillar
and Fatter Caterpillar, that dreamed they lived
on a windowsill under a tree.*

*You couldn't believe how happy they were.
You couldn't believe how fat they were.
They were very fat. And very happy.*

*Until one day an Autumn Leaf fell on the Fatter
Caterpillar to the sinister snip of scissors
and the day went black. Like that:* ☞ ■.
*How interesting. You can't do much under an Autumn
Leaf though, so the Fatter Caterpillar, sensibly,
fell asleep. And in his dream he saw ...*

between the paper & the trees where the sun
gets through between the branches to the grass
under a leaf on a curving stem—the pseudo-fairytale
before the "lyric"/two actors play beforehand too—
how's this? a girl goes by from elsewhere
to set street music its cryptic rhythm against another
how you can live to a different beat an old radio
in a hut on a deserted building site paid little to
live & as to writing/well! but between stations
to pick up the possible & go on with that from there

1

she paces up & down the room. lies down. turns/her love-grief
delicacy in the clammy tropical night. pretends to try to read.
who's that? pale profile in skeletal light through slats. the
wind in the street playacting along with   music

2

gantries through fog enter the city from the port
take the imagination along that track alleyways streets
where nobody not yet chill collar up the script
woodpigeons somehow wads growing with each
breath in yr breast pocket/very popular very human

tight cloth in motion
over the pelvic rhythm. black.
dark the eyes too.
swept past with an eye-kiss
on the street
which they still do
in this city
despite.
which was returned
with thanks   & best wishes

this music goes like this   hollows   twists
pauses developing in places
you follow   then
wonder how it works wonder where I
or as if sideways
to right then   leans
forward into its own   *danger*   against the implications
laughing   back   on the radio/the flickering batteries
of what I have/pressed   & a bit down/well   watching/on the site
the tenacious little details of daily getting by
fog interspersing   as   no   some mist   emphasis
counter simultaneous emphases/bustle in the enclave underground/
& a ghost from another station

Voici ma famille
ma femme
    mon fils   ma fille
et moi.
Je suis Monsieur Legrand.
Ma femme est Madame Legrand.
Ma femme est assise.
Elle lit un livre.
Marie est debout
près de la fenêtre.
my wife the sun the rent
Je suis assis dans un fauteuil.
is due my headache is due
to your headache
Pierre est a genoux sur le plancher
il joue avec son train.
Pierre is screwing
that tart from Kimmage.
Bonjour mon ami.
Écoutez s'il vous plait.

diverge the gaps filling with what may be
who knows look round you that blade noticed
each elsewhere the pages the books the instances
detailed may be dances to your ears as one changes
understanding if you can more music
kitten in the bidet/what did she ever say
our what really is matter to be expressed our
our bright tininess our understandings reticulated
balances go by in the street on fire they look
look at you look at them we meet they-you-I & retreat
parry & plunge & finally at the band where
the waves mesh redissolve where memory &
remembered memories diverge & play over the air
as the air itself is known to play diverging

doing business.
getting the knife in deep & clean
preferably into as many as it is possible
to line up simultaneously in a good
straight voluntary & vulnerable file
(memory) then suppressing the adrenal twitch
to simplify the mind
& steady the hand (memory)
turn hard & true. through memory.
through life. a package deal one says.
to make a killing one says.
   unpredictable high velocity
   confidence in ignorance to be eaten
   hatch in the victim's alimentary canal
   laid in the places frequented by any suitable
   victim species hatch into minute active larvae
   the later stages Collide There are things we meet
   They have nothing to do with/Flash/Don't let it end

Credit all this lumber! Pages. Five hundred books
at least. Shelving (shaky). A desk (ditto). Typewriter.
Erasers. Tipp-Ex, blade, pens, pencils, markers, chalk,
pocket dictionaries—Italian, Spanish, Latin—a
large Webster, C.T. Onions's Concise Etymological,
Dineen's Irish Dictionary, deBhaldraithe's Irish/English,
Garzanti's Grande Dizionario (riddled with curiosities),
envelopes, copybooks, notebooks, paper clips, stapler,
box of staples, a red disintegrating addressbook. The
beginning. There is more. Mug of hot coffee—to get
life moving, tissues—for approaching 'flu, wastepaper
basket, gas fire—turned off: economy in the cold,
bulging folders on which: notes outcrowding notes
aggregating towards a tentative mound: Pieces In Transit,
Odes, Hymns, Notes for Book in Process—uneasy companions,
in process. Various insects would seem to display a similar
madness of aggregation but that even a superficial study
will reveal the logic of. Peep through the ceiling.
Display a man at work! The preliminary foray of a
new entomology. Begin taking notes.

        the trees leaf
        & the leaves shift
        in the air
        figures & machines are passing by
        discontinuously through zigzagged strips
        of sunlight & shadow
        that enzebriate the street outside
        the street
        outside the street
        & it strikes me
glasses   plates   dishes   stray spoons
disorder diminishing   hands warm   racks   shelves
appointed places   the transitoriness in the stormship
a blurred recurrent light in mist.
my daughter playing. quaint notion of permanence!
successive stabbings at the brain-place
peer through the powerful lens beam in
(toothache/earache) everybody home? si, certo, si
    open yr head & gather it all in
    detailing the names faces circles
    railway stations squares a park
    the single rooms circles trees
    stains on the wall sunlight on
    the wall sunlight through leaves &
    branches sunlight on water moving & still
    sunlight somebody combing her hair somebody
    singing whistling watching herself shadows
    rooms places windows names rooms doors
        the release is so fine sometimes
        sometimes   sudden self-anger
        sometimes   blank falling
        I forget the most simple things elsewhere
        wherever my mind elsewhere taking a walk as if
        among very many as if's very
        demanding labyrinthine but I think I
        think lost

odd you know   I still meet them in the street
&   there seems   a new solid film over their features
the mobility calculated now
not quick now with energy   inner/older   masked
I read too much into it or
well   shifty
they're half thinking the same thing
too   *him!*

(As to the bankman who'd fallen asleep balancing a book under a tree beside the windowsill upon which resided our fat, happy and rather clever caterpillars, Fat Caterpillar and Fatter Caterpillar, he woke up when the river—which we forgot to mention—over-ran its banks, and drowned.

And all the fish caught all the money.

Of course it was a great and terrible outrage and the nation mourned. Even Fat Caterpillar and Fatter Caterpillar who'd suffered a change of heart and outlook paused for a moment in the sunlight—two very bright and beautiful butterflies—as a mark of respect to his memory on some tulips on the coffin. Before moving on).

from **Priority**

IN THE MUSIC

The flower of the banana tree is amazing.
Let me say it again: the amazing flower of
the banana tree. Discovering the amazing
flowering banana. Keeping it in mind. Yellow
and purple light in the mind. Ox heart on
drooping penis-like stalk, finger-like
bananas in the heart, growing. On the banana
tree. Those shade-giving leaves. In Lesotho*
the term *banana* in Sesotho means *girls* and
has nothing at all to do with the yellow,
nutrient fruit. *Banna ba bona banana,* "the
boys see the girls," is the music. In the
fruit in the language in flower.

---

* Lesotho, pronounced: Les-utu; Sesotho, pronounced: Ses-utu.

MATURITY

Daybreak: patter of feet to the bathroom and back.
Quiet. Contemplation can come from the toes up
to meet child-energy in the head. Rosettes of
data embed the crystal, shattered similes,
useless blurs but … spalling, advection, cloud-
trails, tidemarks, a swallow in autumn. Mid-day:
bees, wasps, hoverflies tamper at the nectaries I
myself bend to examine looking for stimulation
in the garden. We go out for a walk, my kids and I.
(Fat bananas clustered where the flower was, troughs
and pockets in the head). Life, bright and brief!
Tiny meandering pollen shadows, pocked, minute
circles, diced geometric figures, deeply gouged
brilliant identity-echoes, under the flightpath, up,
wheels dip, flaps down, a steady waver in the great
machine where jets make landfall and go on. My children.
One by one by one. The trees' canopies curl over us,
bend and sway at the sky's lips. Of course. Our
children fly. Fragrance rises. Stem wavers.
World turns. One. Back from the retina shoals of
information slot into place and, from the stone out,
one pollen-grain, one, the fruit's flesh swells.
Delicious! Yellow, the daystar; green is begin.

SOUND

I wish I had a house, wheedle and whine, I wish
I had a bit of money, closing the door,
opening the window. The soul's ability
to ripple through crisp watermarks—vertical
layers—mud and wattle cabins and a tidy
compound. Only a house. In. The.
Breathing. For instance. I wish I had a
roof, my two kids, my one wife. Less
nomadics, but then a whole haversack
of heartstopping examples: wash-basins,
wainscot, rain-pearls on a clothesline,
a clean spread of glasspane deep in its framebed,
whatever you've got, a folded view through
gold and developing veins underground,
small traditional poems—or even less
traditional poems even—or even less.

RAIN

A folder falls open. Isolate and know the details.
Flower-like cup at the shoot apex. Who is running
their wars? With whom am I safe? The child, despite
everything, takes everything in. Be warned.
Then a folder falls open: drained the gear oil sump,
refilled it, bled the brakelines, all set to take wing
on up through Matabeleland. In this heat the Limpopo
all but dry.

A folder falls open: ebony butterfly, blue shocks,
glazed vermillion centipede flowing—elongate—
up a tree. My face pale in a window, at the controls,
eerie glow. Rain and wind. Zooming through hurricane.

And falls to the floor ... flysong, birdsong, cloud-
movement. Sunlight in a stream. The way the water-surface
plaits and pleats. A dragonfly nimble in undersurface
silence though its wings almost never co-ordinate.
My daughter. White gables among trees, leaves bright
and green and dark-veined in the light.

Legislation is the rules of the fight, a rondo in
plot-pages, not a comfort, honey, or didn't you know?
Opulently produced by. Irk and then manipulate. Beware.
Oh?

Deft needle-beak of the weaver-bird flitting bits of
grass through and through into its cosy upside-down
calabash swinging, making for its mate a chambered
showcase. Contact. Otters on their backs in the river

cracking out food. Stones. Gulls crabs another way around.
A monkey's grassblade trickily siphoning living nibblets
from the anthill. Succulent. Flints, axes, arrowheads ...

Then earth quarrelled with sky and sky became
angry and withheld rain. And life on earth began to
dry up and die. Then earth sent a bird to sky
and the bird pleaded with the sky and sky relented
in the end and sent rain. Tentative rain, contending
rain, unbending rain, amending rain, attentive rain,
a tent. Of rain. Question-mark, dart and date. Point,
hack. Circles and arrows. Flint instruments. Needled,
need I say, a stolen music. Not poetry. The point is:
hand over those beautiful garbles. City washed and
scintillant after it, a gully opening up.

SONNET

This is the house I live in now. Dance. Through
data in the Dust Veil Index. Twenty years clothes
waiting in a wardrobe, the wind in the trees cont-
acting in tit-for-tat communiqués, sweat sticky
on the eyelids. What's going on in or who's
winning this game of Pinnacles and Hollows now?

A country uncle sees an imitation African mask
on a windowledge and thinks: Devil Worship.
Precisely. My tunnel is bigger than your tunnel.
In extent, furniture and decoration. Come in.
What's new?

This is the house I live in now. It is to be poor.
It is to be decided on without grounds. It is to
spend one's life thinking, and be thought an idiot;
to live by dint of intensive works, and be thought
lazy; to cherish one's wife and children and
be thought ga-ga. Dance! The grub feeds on the egg,
fat enough then to step down onto the appropriated
honeypool in the cell. See through the delighted
entomologist's eye, delight, discovery. Cracks the
mud-wall, flies free.

In pieces, of a piece, piece by piece, pieced toget-
her, pax. *Do-chum glóire Dé agus onóra na hÉireann.*
And digging at the back of the house—*hah!*—cloud-
bands on the Jovian planets, rusty of-which's, a gnarled
else-tag by the breeze-block wall. Look, wait, I ...

RAIN

Any number of incidents blurring these tiny peaks.
Believing our own eyes watching the image, the
fine film, the regular wedges. Watching what I
see I feel uneasy suddenly because of the. It's
the fragility. It's because Of The Fragility. No-
body else. Tiny dry gulch overhung with palm and
cactus down there. Prickly Pear/Indian Fig in flower
further along. Further along this eloquence gets
dangerous ... History-whispers, emotive mutterings,
do ghlam nach binn. Ash-tree, crab apple, damson,
hawthorn, bramble, the delight spreading, inchmeal.
Click.

That was his life. After so many years away from it
to read again the names in that language, his language,
as any, anybody's, a "dying" language, a braille
following the mind to the spot where your fingertips,
older, colder, bolder, more hungry, descend. To
*nóinín, neantóg, bainne bó bleacht, feochadán, sabhaircín,
fraoch* ... It moves and flits. Bits stay in place.
Bits recombine. Bits underpin then vanish in the argument,
fite fuaite ... *An tosach, ar deireadh.*

Is one negative presented in the dark. The rains
break on the tin roof, peeling a piece of bark to
get the smell of the tree feeding, the imminence of
storms, the next page turning, a flicker of light-
ning—graphite, cork, dust—just as the substance-
strata stagger to the music when everything's evanescent
in its timeblock before going on to pretend that.
That the meaning of meaning (split) matters.

SONNET

You rise of a morning, early, shirt,
underpants, pants, sandals, in the half-
light, quiet. Toilet. Downstairs through
hall, kitchen on tip-toe, through the garden
to the shed at the back of the house
with your bundle of papers. Beginning
is a change of sound and that changes things,
and things tell each other where you are and
how to be and—how do you feel about that?
Blackbird on a wall.

There was a voice, casual, some man
humming some tune, but nobody at all
anywhere about. Later, a little while,
entering a busy street I'm beside a man I
recognize, from years back, humming exactly
that tune, in the fabric, to lock in (out) (as
it were) the extra sense; greedy for that extra,
scavenging at the fence.

.

Luminous beetle, crimson spider, widowbird's long
black kite-tail curving down to cover in the grass.
That birdcall with its weird whistle at the end …
Instep, step. Echo. Undercloud, overcloud pass noise-
lessly in the time of study, head down, from
the heart, the first instructions, *And.* And
going about your business: handedness, symmetry.
That blue in the sky, that white, that off-blue.
But what's this in the shopwindow, ghost-people
connecting with ghost-things shimmering and going by?

IN THE MUSIC

Suddenly I could hear
distinct each wingtap that
a butterfly made quite
clearly quite a way off
coming this way

then about & past again
around my head while the street
I was in to amuse my son
with a racquet & ball
just as suddenly developed

an echo it never before had
taking what I thought I was
saying stopped by a web under a
windowsill the (three-one,
two-four, tap) the/this—

it's in the language, yr pocket,
the back of yr head—silk-dab,
paddle-dip—taking the
sounds & giving them back ship-
shape quietly into the world

where the waters slap & fan:
a pink hand in a red cloth
polishing a brass plate on a brick
wall: *Director of Public Prose/*
"Do you like it?"—

the/this spider failing with its
prey sailing away, music,
dance, winning out again (postbox,
gable-end, walltop) anyway.
Write to me soon. Do.

POINT

Love plants peace. Not a catalogue of manipulative
fairytales. The sky gives back. Gable-shape, tree-lines.
The way the sunlight is, the way it comes down
through leaves, and spider-silk gleams and
doesn't suddenly, between lightly moving branches
in the morning to be still. The order of the stones
in the wall beside the yellow dust-track magnified,
the insect ready, then away over and through a light
dustfall in a sideways breeze gone but, very small,
is noted. *Gósta garbh-Bhéarla:* brief spillage of
birdsong. The first second. The others are different.
The others are written down. *Ah whoom* goes the
orchestra, *spang* goes the Giant's buckle, *wisha-wisha*
go the trees in the grove. Hope, it is hope, and a glow
without a name, Mary, envelops all the places we've
ever lived in, been to, but never—*let the cloning
begin!*—presumed to own.

SOUND

Deep into the furrow of a single underwave
won't give you the sea despite what they say.
They say "corner, corner, corner, corner" …

   crumple up a tissue & dust yr
   desk make a space even the
   paper you write on is damp dhow
   past window starlings on branch
   all this action agitated western
   whiteman with a timetable for a
   spine fiddling about with his
   car its locks & clocks 9 a.m. all to
   a small piece of/head down, at the
   work, when out of nowhere, a bell

     listen: hammer taps
     seam glistens

Item: pencils, pen, desk. Paper. It's good to
see you again this morning, citizens … activists!
Death is nothing. There's the soapstone dish
from Mombasa, the undulant mushroom coral from
Prison Island, Zanzibar. *Item:* in the middle of
November, short, cold days. Pause, detach. Death
is nothing at all. Even among this filthy species.
Item: a window a mesh to test the soul, a door
a blaze of heat and light, burst of energy at the
twigpoint, readiness in the ash-tree's black stops,
pliancy in the toplines down. Down and across …
Close the gate. Close the gate, graciously
close the gate, lovingly, close, ever so, close
it, so, tact, then, do.

LIKING THE BIG WHEELBARROW

We sat on the side of a mountain and muttered
something about the Basotho. We were dissatisfied.
We were given a part of something to understand,
our self-esteem under attack, daily nibblings
at the plinth. Fixing bridges, developing struts.
Wait. The instruction was to wait. Be still.

Dust particles collide and bounce away, collide
again elsewhere and stick until a thicker
filamentary delicate medium sinks to the central
plane of the disk which breaks into rings which
clump and accrete which orbit the core which spark
the beginning of the accretion of the solid cores
of the planets we know, from webs and threads
on magnetic bands. In theory. Only quietest
collisions. Clusters. Crystals and dust grains.
The four-year-old child who said to the pilot
on their way to the plane on the air ferry tarmac:
"I like your big wheelbarrow."

A PERSONAL NOTE

In a laneway
that once was a road
blackberries hang
red & black

the wren in the ashtree
hiding robin abiding
we pick & take home
fruit in a bag.

Over nettles & wet
grass over the hedge &
where birds pass
over the sky

the planet's envelope
& its dead satellite
over this system & its
ordinary star

elliptics spinning, circling,
to a speck my fingers reach in to
one waterdrop tensed from
heaven on a rosehip.

Take it as a gift. Simplify,
condense, know the inside,
dying, travelling towards you
on the track—

coatings of dry spider-bits on the
windowledge—to focus to where
the seam glistens, the hammer
taps. Listen …

AND THROUGH

Bright berry in a blackbird's beak

The sun's risen, condensation on the window.
Intermittent birdcalls. Otherwise so quiet
you can hear my/brush dance (clearly) along
the paper in painting after painting where
I find myself arriving from the other side in,
solar panels glinting (bright berry) against
tympanic black in the vast. Vast ...

bright berry in a blackbird's beak

: the Vast. Maybe I did see what that contained, once.
Remember. Rotate. That did include the sea. Spin.
As it happens. Round. On a red dust track tired
and repeating the simple in fatigue of heart and
fatigue of spirit, repeat, the simple pattern.
Involve. Stone outcrops, flat sky. Task: draw close.
Make hope. Don't die:

bright berry in a blackbird's beak.

In time, nothing. Love, work, knowledge. The weapons
are nothing in deep time. In through the eyes, ears—
wing-caressbeats over the landscape—braided rivers—

bright berry in a blackbird's beak.

People have houses. Spaces. People occupy spaces,
radial spokes connect, fold, knot. Conduits, taps,
struts. Their difficult obsession Labelling the Clouds
equals what, however?

   Bright berry in a blackbird's beak

.

Each shock each minim of each thing here
cored chord cordate current
a life a labyrinth of glistening
inconsistencies but to *keep* that   kept
each bright at-least each tooth in the zip
each strange thing   its lenticular glow in the distance
a strange thing   bright berry ...

   bright berry in a blackbird's beak.

from **Steps**

IN THE MUSIC

When the leaves wither and begin to blaze and
fall all the way down the ladder to each
rootweb's radius in a plot they make a brittle
miracle of beginning a paintbox on the bright grass,
the die set. There it is, in the slack between
one of the little stopped waves on the tin roof
over where I know its nest is in under the beam
over the window, flea-hunting. Quick-quick, gone.
Log: at the Problem Wall at the heart of the maze,
do not impose your will.

Being all ambiguous cloud-places and so quiet so/
that *is* there could be thought to/I think they/
what's that? trickle on the map, a musaic, (could
be an omen, I mean, amen) cloudberry and hare's-tail
cotton grass, "messages come in flashes", ready or
not. Nonetheless. Perhaps. However. Argument.
Disputation. Dichotomy. All circles, glints that in
the cross-grain/skarns/revert; do not impose your will.

Is it really the 10th? Can't be. Wait a minute. (So
many facts, so much manufacture, so little prey.)
Tipply-pip, says the bird, *do-you-agree, do-you-agree.*
Sometimes, briefly, even here I/or/I do. But then ...
A cat in the grass, amity, seedcup.

MARCHING SONG

Tittle on the drum. A seated figure
at a desk from the back. A ten shun.
A tube of dust. Descending steps. In
sum. It's. It's the way they're always
"they" and never ever ever. Ever.

Plant your feet on the ground as the
basis evaporates in a blur of academic
backchat/I think I/Got that? Turn round.
As if as if as if …. The point of the
story, the point of all his little stories
was, note, *poor me*.

.

As if the running could ever stop anyway,
each sour step collecting bitterness at each
failure to pause to close the spaces between
things and their settings, selfish, lazy, blind,
deaf, never growing up, never wanting to,
even their own children sacrificed to
particularly their own children sacrificed to
this ego-dark, this maw. Is the point.
How do you feel about that? Close the book.

Daystar on a branchtip, raindrop holding in.
They'll come, they'll succour and lay siege,
furtive and uninvited in the early hours,
vanishing in a cloud of ionised futures busy
under the sun beginning. Dry sticks, foot-
prints in the dust.

.

(A) Walk away, and their weapons are gone;
laugh at yourself (B) and they bury themselves
in their own muck. Let everything, as it
happens, (C) happen between brackets, and the
brackets (dreaming) bulge, skip, loop.

The sun *block* the moon; the night *block* the day;
winter-spring-summer *block* the autumn top; tap trowel,
scrape. The gap between the footsteps on the stoep.

IN PRAISE OF PAINTING DOORS
for Louis' recovery

If your five-year-old son falls from a high wall
to concrete and fractures his skull, concentrate
your love. Focus everything. Everything. Everything,
day and night. Everything.

Afterwards, all going well, leaving the hospital,
take brushes and white spirit. Everything. Don't
underestimate the virtù of the clean rag in the pocket.

White can be a bore, that's true.

On the other hand, a whole lifetime can be a foil (too).

That the confluence/congruence of colours in the world
has something to do with the pulsebeat of blood in the
human body might be worth looking into. But not yet.
Hell! *Rag*.

At waist level, sit and paint to your patient boot-top.
The spine deserves pleasure too, not panic, not despair.

Don't be proud of your house. Obviously ... The jackal
solicitor has his fangs in your neck. And there's the
little matter of deep time. Paint on.

Walls speak to doors. Doors answer back. However much
tempted, never intrude.

In the hallway. In the living-room. Oh, and here's one:
in the 'utility room'. Now where do *I* live?

My children's feet in their shoes on the floor.

Fly with the positive possible energies landing only
to watch in delight.

You too were something once.

Return brushes to spirit. A force in the body of the work
demands it. Sit, eat. Ash-tree sapling outside in the play-
breeze by the window.

Having shed clutter, to the next house go, with a light
pocket, a light heart, a light touch, a fire in the mind,
and a plan, lightly carried, as lightly let go.

FIRE

Moving through shadows under trees,
diamonds and islands of light sliding over
a figure disappearing into the dark,
the closely-felted interlocking needle-like
crystals of feldspar with a scattering of
colourful smaller crystals of olivine
and pyroxene and some black specks of
iron oxide/then one. Sharp. Jab. Move,
if you dare. Before you start anything,
stop.

The magic mice make gold. The beautiful
poor girl's hair is gold. The boulder rolls
from the cave's mouth disclosing gold.
Gold, gold. There is gold leaf to each tree
and a rich vein under the forest imminent.
Then I woke up.

Rest your head in your hand. Task: (still)
fill in the spaces between the waves of
that echo. Draw close. Opal. The mango fills
your palm and weights it, scrupulous, before
you bargain, before you speak, before you
breathe again, calm.

PERMISSION

who, diabetic, prone to gangrene, lost both
legs   bit by bit

whose family abandoned him

whose wife realigned

whose case was taken up

who arrived back suddenly from the hospital
in a wheelbarrow

who was constrained to sleep separately

whose gable collapsed in the rainy season but
seemed nonetheless content to live thus till
his son came back from the mines   a tidy
compound & a hard wife

who employed himself with us one day out of the
blue under a tree cutting the branches he could
reach for kindling for tobacco money & just never
afterwards quite went away

who got about with chunks of tyres on his stumps

who never missed a party at our place

who must have watched me sit my young daughter
on the slowly disappearing wooden fence of our compound
(quality firewood) of an evening for a chat

whose son came back from the mines in the end &, drunk,
thanked us   florid & a little, somehow, threatening

.

so.

that Threads can intersect at the dead mesh of

Poignancy (yellow dust at my feet, blue
mountains, far sky) (I am quite sensible
to this) if let.

& yet.   so.

RESPONSIBILITY

Washing her clothes in a rusty
old wheelbarrow by the dam by the
track under the eucalyptus where
frogs at night fill the village
air with/her bright brown eyes
and mouth connect in a smile whose
radiance and playfulness the fine
skin black/I thought I could get to
know almost everything once not quite
yet feeling the bounce in the net
(The Oxford English Dictionary of
Spraints, The Pretoria Encyclopaedia
of Mortgages, The Concise Cambridge
Political), when arcane thinking
clicks in its conduit. Tap: "an artist
is *never* poor." Swallow that.

RAIN

then cut this wood   with care   following its line
ply & tooth   the weapons are nothing   mind yr hand
keep time   cutting true & crude   then

tacked it   silver through yellow   a whole mountainside on fire

webshadow/masterstrand   affix, set by, scoop & try   shedding what
(little insect on the page) writing writhing riding
the waves' more basic music trebled, trembled   allows

& dreamtracing (the weapons are nothing) the array   a
light in the language   a light for the language
alighted in the dust of a hilltop village   the weapons   which

                    is the flower you
                    can grip this flower with
                    extreme care

                    once   are nothing

                    clicks & ululations …

the smoky homework of my students

the hopeful homework of my students

the struggle in the homework of my students

the pathos in correcting the sad, smoky homework
of my students

                    … big, braided rivers.

STEPS

a

driving in a red dustcloud
for hours years wandering
wondering how to

connect

this stone to that hut with
precision tact   two hands one
gift   wait listen   right
left   shimmering elastic

wallhome
(not any other barrier
but a breeze over it)
welcoming.   conduit.

b

blue flower   strong stem
oval stone in the stream

I was stepping lightly home
(the baby developing)

starlings' jabber-click
cutting with the burin nick

conical hills   stone outcrop
two swans   one rooftop

dead flower   dead stem
dead stone in the stream

a fish shadows by. a cloud.
a bird. wake up, coward.

c

window lit
fire in the grate
door closed over
table set

food being ready
ready the appetite
(in dreams begin steadi-
ness) come, sit—

peeling a piece
of bark to get
the smell of
the tree feeding—

when threads mesh as they cross
over they sing to us.

this is how to live.

FOUR CORNERS

PASTORAL
    Skin of the earth on the
    earth   fragility

    agility
    profusion of bud-plans

    of   &
    blot   manoeuvre   corrode

    do I/we/you/they
    have to repeat even more
    more?

    It's
PASTORAL
    When grasslands disappear
    & the slopes are denuded

    the topsoil
    without grip

…the finial pit
    of the first recorded

    raindrop

    bangs
    the tympanum.

    Let
PASTORAL
    Small wave-like motion of
    sound/someone singing

in a radio in a
kitchen over a

hedge on a windowledge
somewhere not far off.

Some bits
of words of
interest

or is it a
woman singing

outside the radio
her heart out?
PASTORAL
    Valleys, villages, coastline. A map
of a stain on a wall. Alive & living,
not a crammed glasshouse of pistillate
verba. Grass bends back. The book
is fat, contains code. The world,
the water planet. The code contained in
this thing in the world, the book, changes
the things, the world. Elytral sutures
open & wings, surprising & beautiful,
begin to work. The point is. Fernbrush,
nervure of such wings, small pebble
adjustments. Song.

FIRE

i.m.: Paul Klee

A

suddenness of what snow does
to a doorstep when you
wake to it in the morning
early before almost anyone

(& why the verb *to be*
in so many languages
at such an angle should be
so irregular so often)

a slate gone there
emphatic & there too
yes the wind blew this way
not that when

(is a mystery to me.
where were you when they
named the name of money
in your name anyway?)

the snow fell graphic many
ways across you (curls joinctures
loops stops) to make the black & white
unmelting music of what is

B

being coiled into a deft, modified past
not in money-work but secret
difficulties darkness pleated

dovetailing deeper dark down to
an all-dimensional ground blackness
being coiled into a deft, modified past
hollowing, carving, cutting (I went out.
I met nobody/I came back. faced it.)
the greedkeep, health, sanity, calmness where
the roots are, coiled, magnified,
crystal spindles at the branch-heads,
spasm of light

        a wind that
        turns a leaf on
        the ground or
        ientate
        yourself.

        .

        grey black
        stone ochre.
        grey black
        ochre clay.

        .

some monumental crap about gathering honey
in the tympanum of a bank's façade
small waterplanet tubby patriots
the minim of "known" history, vertical siphon, pip.
dogfish upriver, another world
light through glass touching the light
curtain reflected on the tabletop surface
upside-down repelled
returns—
pax! paxpax! pax!

goes the fighting in the street
being coiled into a deft, modified past.

        •

        grey black
        ochre stone
        grey black
        ochre clay

        •

C

a triangle of sun
light on the
wall of a
shed.
    blue sky. join the
    dots. child-wit.
    the blue plane.
    the blue
    plane
draws the eye
along then
down to
chim
    neys & rooftops. here
    we are. slightly
    closer to the
    heart
of creation (but still
not close enough)
at the base of
an old tree
(minute

      grains of white quartz
      imprint of the nail
      in the mud &
      webbing bet-
      ween 3
toes & mare's tail sprung from ooze
a spider web, ready) a small
bird buried. even that.
the tune complifact
scraptured.
      five seagulls in V-form-
      ation & a quick
      sparrow too
      makin a
      mane.
it's wonderful to wake up sometimes
to the feeling of time in the morning
early, crisp, moving for a moment in
the first day always, clasp & bars
of the metal gate in the hedge outside
(say) by the pathway where—can do on
contact—the garden—you are—a glass
of cool water on a sunlit sill—intricate
tickle on the face—bright berry—the air
puckered where the silkseed drifts *that*

held to the Waiting Posture, *that* music an instant
fit to stave only an order in a sea of which/&
orders. when a token's taken & returned
fluent—"beautiful ideas for prov-
iding truth"—a *legal-decision-*
trial-peace pouch in waiting
(pat)

   clé deas
     you could ex-
  plain
          Peru
release the Trees
   Animals
           Engines
 joining the
    Geometric Dance
on a shed wall
         of an evening
  vertical to the *why* in yr pockets
 (otherwise empty you go about with
   proud & prim nonetheless)
  mirrors gaps branch-formations
   the very sight in the head—
     conical hills
    stone outcrops—
staving off all aggressive parasites
 & ear to the beat of breathing
  returned renewed & singing
     why
/whirring pipsqueak/can't-thinking
  why can't thinking
   fit thinking fit
   this apt
   black black
   grey red
   black red
   grey grey
    black

    ·

from **Adherence**

| A |

BALLAD

. .

Stop.

Walking through
leaves on a hilltop
was being will in

balance tell valency that
chance is a hand (step)
spread in the light, see

shade you don't
dread/thread where
you are/a long

time thing
shining
but

not a word

nervure of a fly's wings
to blur the lens, difficult,
working through, watching,

taking note, watching, puzzled,
delighted, in a presence
(never anything by rote)

beyond sense, sentient.
Black green
blue

all of the welkin well despite any
petty personal grouch under your
spreading canopy and—

pick an apple from a tree,
apologize—

like a bird
flit but

not a word

difficult. The broken
pieces, the spoken
pieces,

fleet mother
of like-
ness

twisting a glass
in a tunnel

the whisper-movement in the grass,
quill-scratch, trickle-piece
(click) but/The speed,

the light, the space. Even your next
conception of the. Height. Of a.
Glass wall stops.

Not it. No. Move … a long life and
a quick death brushed by the
rhythmic wash of the rain

the rule is the pieces to wait for
the right moment
the pieces

the echo-places where the
smooth spaces
between

the eye of the net and the eye
waiting and taut
and

a love of watching a flower
matching the sun's face
following

a blackbird's silhouette on the last
branchtip, note-bits finely
mapping the place/but

—clouding, clearing, clouding—
does teaching *really*
exist?

—stop—stand back—let me see—not a word—

ripples slip across the
surface of the glassy
water where

the flat stone dropped from
its flight from
me

                    to mark the spot in the lake
                       with precision
                          tact—

site normal, nothing to report.
Cling to the lattice
in

a shattering rain of
names
and

part-names beaten out of/eaten
out of meaning,
house, home

and that planned future
mortgaged to your
systematic

Friend at the Bank downtown as
the Furniture Beetle's
audible

rasp over your head under
your very nose
busy/but

not a word—

                    stopped

              ink to the paper dancing
              vanished thy besy praier
                    in speciall

lift up your heart
and sing

*wingflash/finprint/loves-in-
the-storm/between
minūte*

*& brief, & back,
the leaf arguing with the light*

where rock splits in a palace
of despair-places, shock
of mountain avens

taking my pen thinking to
put it down again
often

and pausing to having the real
eyes for and still not moving
a nearly not knowing yes

a lightning chrysalis

acrobatic
bright
cone

to the centre (infoliate,
quiet) of quietness, quietness
giving way to quietness

opening, entered,
spring/neap.

Drop.

. .
.

| B |

Tree-
touch, air-
waves, leafmark.
Step. A guide may be
indentations in the tree, if you
need a guide, a grip. Step. Not
ever again not any admonition or
any song. The term laid stark and
the edges precipitous.
Step. Which terror can you dare
choose to ingest first? It all
could be worse. *La vitesse* in life,
L'espace in hope of peace in place
and your life placed at the
border and the border de-
fined. Step. To the
top, fluent, and
from there, to
begin.

I had a pot of white paint on a red ladder
and was painting the kitchen window
in a cool breeze on the last day of May.
Slight pain in the head. Glancing at a fly
on the wall. Birthday, for emphasis. Fact:
to dislike the walls of the cave. Stuck.
Fact: cool breeze. Fact: old red shirt.
Hop on your bike to fix your fyke, keeping

each new silly surface clean beside a
breeze-block wall, a game of boxes in the
Late Upper Holocene. First the small one for
the narrow edge. Then the wide one for the beam.
Dip. Fact: where one stone touching another
stone in the dark in silence in the tower where
lichen spreads at its own speed on the light-side
and a spiral staircase won't stop going up.
Stop. Stone. I'm not/or/I'm waiting in that
space where Black keeps eating White,
a philosophy of craving, a trick the reaper
likes repeating—pliant tube, tufted frond—
a way into the delicate fossil-music,
dark, light, indigo, coral, that won't leave
my daren't my ear alone. Life is. Ever more
briefly, bright. Sit. Giggle-blather. Tell
                nobody. Dip.

C

...

Rest, happiness, peace in discipline
take water for instance a passerby
stopping for music & good food yes
the sound of the water the river but
that which can't be described.

...

A fly cleaning itself precisely
by the window in sunlight
forelegs back (rest) head eyes
shadows wings brittle-quick & quite
like writing really. Out there. That.

...

of every person who would be a party to
a conveyance to the fee simple free from encumbrances
of the property described in the schedule hereto attached
buzzed the/flash/by the glass disappearing sideways
into a or in the direction of

>   at least a
>   pentad of
>   *(on top of*
>   *the world*
>   *the air thins*
>   *out & heaven*
>   *laughs)* trees

...

Rest happiness peace old
pain-in-the-head (mica-fleck,
cricket-click, a black & white
flash, five-fingered flower on
the cave wall) vanishing &
glinting in the triple breeze.

...

Intricate walking (happiness)
down the laneway with the twins
small house—by a river—
lesser celandine, wild strawberry
in flower. Just love. Nobody wins.

...

Your wooden ladder of As-If to play with. *Hah!*
Actinic. Up steps. One one one one one.
That circle of coincidence that brought you
here from Africa to capture tourist brochures
of the soul for a season for a song that.
Don't look back. Or

down. The ant moves the grain. The ant disappears
underground to come back again with a grain.
The ant moves the grain then disappears underground
again to get another grain to build and/click/
it goes down there through other into the dark
to get more and. The grains allow themselves to
be touched. Slap. Touched by elaborations for
what archaic quillities, the code, the children
giggling by the river, duck, past, gone, clarity
holding the sky (bridge) up holding the sky up, too
(stone). One one one one one.

Down
goes the machine down
through a steel chute
black diagonal shadows
marking a regular pattern pacing
its controlled descent with a whirr
and a click as—down—close your eyes—
pip goes a car in the street far—as may be—
away *pip-pip* in response meaning: The World
is all that is in phase—meaning:— down—
The eare is a rational sence—down—and
certain—meaning: a chiefe judge of proporcioun

            too

adding (down) leaning to the law that
each thing its number its place
between the/ *because* of the shadows
interlocked and separated figures
things missing or things wedged side-
ways that remind us that all orders
have their justification in the end in
an order of orders only our faith as
we work, addresses—oh!—
slows down and stops to lock level with a
click: door-grid slides back …

        Dust rising from the track
        where the dance started
        in the heat, concentrating each
        tap on the tympanum,
        travelling elsewhere how
        shadowbits, lightsplashes—
        pick an apple from a tree—

a door, a desk, a window,
a crude thing for anyone
to hide in over the years
maybe …

COHERING
Sudden Glory

SETTING

Look
it entered the shed
through a
crack under the
closed door
following then
sending up
sun-hungry leaf
for life to vie
till it found
well nothing
particular to
grow around so
turned (look) back.
To the sun. Settled.
All those books
& nowhere to go?
"Yr life will be
  full of happiness
(marks in snow
 show snow-negatives
 in grey-white
 blackwhite) happiness"
say the Bones. I see.
Pens, blue then
red. Bind
bound bindweed

found wine-seed
lime green
life-road twined
in triple flight
to fall to land
ground-side up,
under the sun.
Young pup
that you've
always been
prefiguring
a print
in rock
the print.
The rock. Knock.
Whether it wither
in this weather
  or not, going back
    against the
      books
the dance of rain
snow   discovery
taking in   letting
go   molecular pavanes
in rings & chains
    pistons   combustion
reading   doubt
    day/night checkerwork
cloud-dance   tidal-
dance   dance of the whale
    ants & bees   dance
of the binary
systems   dance of the
regenerating

lithosphere   things
in relation   rippling
wing-edges
dance of energy
dance of the
blood
    the dance
of the
    blood
slow sets
   shimmering nets
mountains
   moving.
   So.

Open the door,
step in, wipe feet,
leave the mat,
walk to the chair

by the desk, switch
on the lamp & the
heater for a bit too,
sit down, start.

Everybody's busy,
en route, clickity-clack,
but what you have
in the cave

one slim green
    arrow
my hands bare
filicoid stellate

waterpieces that
diffuse to the
surface wait
the chip-glint

in the rock that
cuts through cuts
  through cuts
    despair

bird all-forgetting bird designate bird shimmering
    Despair.

There is a cold solar haze. There is smoke.
And blue. And gold. Emphatic branchtangles,
angles of (Victorian) chimneypots, rails,
wires, traffic, the pouring canal by Newcomen
Bridge. An impossible accent placed in gay paint
there over the P in *Oifig an Phoist* by
Newcomen Bridge. *Éist! Éist liom!* Ghostlanguages
of herofurniture. Even here, dipping into
yr bag, lips pursed, eyebrows raised, sound of
the guttural morse of the swallow.

I was crossing a street when it struck me
suddenly—lights changed red—it came from
a wave from one of my books into Mountjoy Square
where the air was rolling back in front of it.
(Daddy, Daddy what's yr book?) (Oh that the
anthropoid's too fussy today we can't but agree:
I love myself & you love me. But I so love
another for her delicate grace I can't peel my
bananas or pick the nits from yr face.) Set
Thing Ring Net. The twig snaps. Waters that/that
fatten to an icicle. Echo of axe coming down
on wood—pale bole, dark ground—under whose
shade the ant takes a grain, the replicate grain
tapped in—smart, accurate—below ground.
Palp. Here I am. Peace is a small house by a river.
Sound of the water. A cobweb in yr doorjamb
in the morning after dew. Splits the world in
rainpools ... Daddy? I made a song in a murderous
time. Listen to the sound of that.

AND DESPAIR

A quiet
chipping draws
my attention back
to the window where
the laws of tension
*The poetry of despair
is blank. Sit. Quote.
Birds fly, tie down
the birds.* Mind darkens,
rock splits, head
blazing, hands hope-
less in place of
splinters where the laws
of listening & the laws
of tension meet
the laws of light …
to fight it out
in whispers.

    listeners there
      are &
    steady hey but

    cohere? go there
look: hanker after
    people or a

      god or a blinding
        pattern
      one of the

  smallest birds in
the world its
  nest the size

    of half a
      walnut shell
    built to such

    deft such delicate
these feathers
    leaves even telltale

     flower-petals moss
       hair feet
     bill spider-thread

    weaving or the
bird's own saliva
    together or both

    dancing in despite of even

        out over
        the mimosa flicker
        past the village to
        the mountains

their eggs even
    their eggs themselves
stuck down fast

against gales one
flat yes precision

      stuck down
        fast.

       . .

Good. To have invented
happiness. To have to
re-invent it

under stress. Sit down
stand back/filament
filament

feathery the web in the flue that's
held this house up for
so long for

you for instance so
pliant so desper-
ate

so long the
smoke
says

(fringed with mystery just
 beyond the splash
 zone)

so long
as I
can

(*now* I
 know
 oh)

tiny multiple
rivetings
I

(can't quite/Love
as a garden
escape?)

(dog in a hurry leg up
tail erect off again
busy) quite

grip it/the shaking shadows
of the dead when
sifted/

that plastic bag that
spits & whispers in
the breeze

"... *Spirit?* What do *you* know
about poverty
of spirit

anyway? For comfort & luxury
a cinch to swindle a
lyric poet or two

(for instance) with a vulnerable
brother to boot for
instance

when the strong players die
get senile or otherwise
out of the way

& the dice collide. Listen.
Listen just slip into
action within a day

or so of burial pretending
caritas-loving-concern
to the place where

the hinges singe & the money burns
& hey presto. Lick, twist.
The light. Ethical?

Rubbish! This is how it works, this
is Life spinning on its
radical pretence:

an old bone in every family—the Weak
shall inherit the Dearth, the
shadows. Surely you know

that? Stand back.
Gouging pretty
messages

on the Church-Bank door—
there goes Michael
rowing his

bloody boat ashore again & good
riddance (Alleluia)—now
that I think of it

is yr cup of tea, isn't it?
Delicate-
ness

art & significance
& all that.
Get a job.

I just thought I'd pass it on
for what it's worth sonny,
a little bit of light

on embezzlement & misery.
You don't get the
picture? Then

   don't be *in* it.
   Stand back ... "

  Oh

the Cockatrice Greed-in-Life Rampant
   Gules.

  Good.

Pasture. Sky. Bird.
Time to go. Time-time.
Some sound. Sound-sound.
Steps. A wall. Sun. Instar.

Barred bead along the string
(call) continuing meets the
stopped bead at the other side to

/tick/should it/might it/but …
counts. Then nouns then verbs.
      Are.

    Bright sun bright
    white wall fine
    flowerhead blazing
    red. Tally. Bright.

    Sun bits. Blue light.
    Green butterfly. Gold
    pupa. Shadow-
    sound. Oh right.

        Cut
        through
        that
        too

TO THE

Ten thousand
intent at desk the
in stopped swirl
the ten thousand
things that convene
shine escape
intermittent material
in a pipe that
& that dying out. Half
a walnut
a shell.

Whereat the root
music of the unpat
threads means to/
then but/

CUT

Alive to the slapped silver & black
water & sunlight a lime tree twig
versatile against gales gone into the
upper layer & stuck down fast in a fault
in the mind in need of repair even leaves
that angle back to listen to the beginning,
harmonies bathèd in charm in a cave
somewhere, cohere. To stick down fast
one flat, yes, precision.

Let's see: glue to the web. *Cast yr nets
before the jelly sets.* Be warned.
Don't despair. *It's a tradition, bits of
attrition.* Short breaths, in small space,
second thoughts, first steps, in April
& replete, begin. Forget. *A web is a
crowd of kisses.* Ah. Chuckle in the locks.

A ballad, knocked flat, someone in the
memory, frantic to be back. Forward: dis-
appear into the multiple glint of twisting
arabesque (with point). Up: blank. Down:
blank. To the sides: blank. Alive & breathing
—swim, reptile!

SMILE

Sudden Glory
is the passion
which maketh
those
Grimaces
called Laughter.*

Ever. And ever after.

*Thomas Hobbes

THE GEOMETRY OF SOAP BUBBLES

A hot cuppa in a cold shed, a wintry blast
outside & far away in Endwhile unbelievable
rumours of peace among the nectar suckets ...

        .

only a few rules & those/to pick
a step here a thumbprint there
to twist it into pieces until
crystal specifics splinter against
        chary when given what might be
        what/bulloney (the key?) ...
got a job mornings setting up oilcans
governed by a few elementary
weighty five litre cans in navy
silver screwcaps three pyramids on
three pumps
        & two as proud under the window
        Esso—yes O/*they can form are*
        governed by the few the rules
        my hands *can be shown*
the till had a moneysmell
to be self-healing with respect to
small punctures paper & sweat I suppose
& continued Living too edge to edge
the locks (no) still can't click (pert) open
        or just watching the laburnum flare
        & snow on the lawn opposite (who can
        tell what it is explores a madness
        in a man Mary anyway hey & you know
        me) stuck in this honeycomb scribbling
        away

pawning the bloody typewriter again
& a few other Elementaries borrowed
for the occasion *the geometry
of the possible* the blurred vertigo
the quick breathing the special pleading
& still patch
     Monday to Friday putting in the
     weddingring & the iron given the
     sensibility to receive them as
     lights change red yr number please
     (dog sniffing wet stain on black
     tyre of black hearse) (empty glinting
     exoskeletons in the multiple traps
     in the grass *tinkling* in the light
     vast trawlsock)
& run out of busfare too a dab
at borrowing by this time *can come
together* despite *in only two ways*
knowing well the rules that
equalled the incapacity to move
through configurations yr friends
extend in yr regard with
     love flash of tail-feathers
     (scribbling) downright-fangled
     Love O it was a happy life
/chary/or care fernlike
starlike *The possible
configurations governed
by a few elementary rules
that have been
     known for more than a
     century. This new mathematical
     model provides a sound*

basis for those rules.
A sound basis for those
rules. Sudden glory.
Blueprints as to use
on the walls
                of caves, the makers' instructions'
                magic magic still, splinters that
                light a winter window echo
echo the little finger,
ring, middle, index,
knucklejoints, thumb, palm,
wrist, deep in the world,
open, touching.
                Look.

"*The possible configurations they can form are governed by a few elementary rules that have been known for more than a century. A new mathematical model provides a sound basis for those rules ...*"

from 'The Geometry of Soap Films & Soap Bubbles' by F. J. Almgren Jr & J. E. Taylor (*Scientific American,* July, 1979)

from **Postlude**

from **FORGETTING EVERYTHING**

The tree beside
the water's
standing

still—the water there
is standing too or
seeming to

though full of little dark
& darting things
& fluctuant.

The bird is in the tree
the wind its briefly
on a branch

beside a leaf I see
twice then flies
back

over the ranch
to the
cliff.

The farmer is walking
across the dust
of the ranch.

Ridged bootmarks
in the dust of
the ranch.

The sky of this place
is blue. And justly
famous.

One two. An envelope of
useful chemical
reactions.

Cut down too on yr
tobacco intake.
One four.

Reaches the landrover. The Tree.
The Stream. The Bird.
The Cliff.

Water moving by in the stream
here has many fine
characteristics.

Look. Bird reaches cliff.
Fenugreek folding its
leaves

around its wedge-flower.
Lebanese?
Sundown.

Moonlight.

Living in a world where
things happen
someone

will play the viola
someone will &
someone

will &—counting
on it—a
large

crimson spider—a
small silver
gimmick.

Tearshaped apple-
seed moist
mahogany—

one two four/one
two four
three—

presence & pressure
of space—one's
future—

boundless periods of stillness
curling gradually
so that

each dream congruent
into the next
continuing

solo in the shadows under
the leaves out of the
sun in Sleepy Hollow.

Intricate mist building
on a window-
pane.

Four kittens lap milk
from a tray on
the ground.

Four apples in a
row on the
windowsill.

Arithmetic (Plato) *has a
very elevating
effect.*

from **Sonata**

A SONG
(& A DANCE)

i.m. Ric Caddel

Remember that clematis
plant Ric brought us here to
Dublin dug in by the new
place in flower now on
a wall in spring
mindful of how it goes
in quiet radiance as all
does worth the caring for—
tag to Ric's tact and
a reminder.

.

Remember that clematis
limber through lattice
in flat ice flowers
on a wall
being spring in
this climate growing
in radiance beyond all noise
as everything does
worth the caring for—
tag to Ric's hand
and a reminder. Grace.

.

Remember that clematis
climbing in silence
twisting limbs through
tacked lattice embered
everywhere in flat
shockflowers on a wall
being spring in this.
Yes. Stays.

.

Trembling clematis
(its crowded flowers, its
teeming greens) in a light
breeze now set out that
year Ric came to visit us
by the south-facing wall
mindful of how it shows
in quiet radiance
bits of evidence too
complex to hold still and
still not see through that
end-beginning nonsense to
the no-frame of life beyond
our lives—tag to Ric's plant.

A reminder. And a dance.

...

left out bin
clapped hands
dog slips in

closed windows
plugged the kettle
in touched the tree

nod again decide
again negotiate
the gate

the railings
& all that inhale
exhale bus goes

by cleared up
table then around
a pebble drops in

time have you noticed
ice glass kids at
school around

then about bus
down street cross
the floor the mat

slipped off shoes
                     dance

angle of the house
mirror doorway stair-
well hey! around &

then/clap hands
tap the tap the sink
step architrave

my notes yr song
quotes fall from
the air all dance

take this from that
put those there
return to begin

again gain grace by
degrees only watch
yr step there &

practise here | you
are holding yr breath
here the air gives

back its light to
spare here fear
is falling into the

past all dance glint
   dancing away

/ ...

    where
        is
the
        tree
bent
        severe-
ly
        to
the
        left
I
        remember
(it)
        below
me
        as
I
        write
a
        not
a
        power
a
        birch
black-
        ened
by
        traffic
gives
        small
green
        leaves
this

      slice
of
      bright-
ness
      in
the
      just-
begun
      over
the
      black
rail-
      ings
in
      the
garden?

cars.

a
      dog
bark-
      ing.

sirens.

a
      bus
stops

all danced
all dance away

...

Around a loose thread and

> remember that clematis
> plant Ric brought us here to
> Dublin dug in by the new
> place in flower now on
> a wall in spring—

have a cup of tea I said.
have a cup of tea. I think
I will. I did. (the circle's
an intriguing totem.) stir it.
and start again.

ah-ha! *they said peering*
down at the specimen in a
circle round the table

   stone circles   literary circles
     circles under the eyes

> —twisting through its
> lattice emblems everywhere
> trembling teeming in a
> light breeze mindful of
> how it goes when it goes
> to bits our lives mistakes
> radiance—a limberwort—
> it is—yes, this—and

failing tags or evidence—
mind my moustache—what's
new?—little understood.
so very little understood.

remembering that clematis
plant Ric brought us here ...

SONG

On the field of beginning
a ripple hits a ripple
where the cat barks
and the dog denies it
over the other side
of a wall over there

but here you sit and listen
where Do Not Grab
is tacked to your shed
and leaves move in a light
breeze in a sideways light.
Spider: beware.

The angle of repose
and the angle of agitation
fuse together at base
to build a place from
nothing and go on.
Do not grab.

It's Istin isn't it—
for a high level of confidence
& oedema, headache, flushing,
dizziness, nausea, fatigue,
palpitations, somnolence,
abdominal pain, altered

bowel habits, arthralgia,
asthemia, dyspepsia, dyspnoea,
gingival hyperplasia,
gynaecomastia, impotence,
increased urinary frequency,
mood changes, muscle cramps,

myalgia, pruritis, rash,
visual disturbances,
erythema multiforme,
jaundice & hepatic enzyme
elevations …
in the field of beginning

to draw a line in the snow
melting into each side
of the argument
on the side of the mountain
before arriving where
you'd not intended to go:

a bit of lyric goes a long long way
so on our way back from
that place a glow—& a sting.

Now, Devonex for children too.
You'll like the way they like it.
Local irritative papular eruptions.

Leaves—needles—cones—
after the storm the storm's work
& birds sing.

It's Istin, isn't it?

Honey, I'm home.

SONNET

then I woke up.

paring a pencil
carefully, its
frill, its dark

dust, a fly's
shadow rubbing
its forelegs
together

by the
window

green
blue
red

(thank you for that)

bees
shad
pine-trees

rats in the tube
hi! cherryjam please

yes not a word into
the fabric favours
privileges safeties
mesh & fix/not step-

ping lightly over
the cobbles/of the
piazza through
the fog—

& clipped my nails
with pleasure &
gathered thinking
the sharp-pointed

curves cut with
pleasure thinking
together into a
little heap

(

)

momentary picture
of birds in flight
over ocean & tipped
them into the

wastepaper basket
beside me with a
small fillagree
of ticking sound—

home now to my papers
in silence in a box
godwot _____

_____

foam

                                    ice

bale

    castor

blunt as that—
    to live
watching
    never expecting to
participate

or directly anyway
    dimple a surface
tilt an
    event to yr will
set the date

on the page
    start
startled
    shifting sideways
again where

all the little
    pieces fall

black.
a dot. a
dark dot
moving

hang on
a sec a
spider
quiet in

a corner
sound of a
bee at its
abc

scraping a
nectary rain
on glass to
the side of

yr face as it
sizzles is
it & back to-
wards each tiny

towards each
tiny percussion
the word for
"word" write

down look
up excise
you play I
play tin op

ener in yr
hand of an
evening
cook talk

sketch need
ing to rel
ax dancing
needing I

suppose I
is that a
question?

is that
Goodie-Two-
Shoes at
the door.

jaggeds.
oh sure.
a cushy
number

for the
peccable
each mouth
moving

someone
else's
greed-
focus

snapping
neatly into
each clear
prediction.

I saw the
word *variegated*
follow the
curved

line subtle
over the
pebble's
smooth

to its cut
reservoir
at the side
there

asper. the
word *time*
the word
pity.

that's the
end of the
argument—
a bubble

of plusses
floats pops
in the half-
dark with

a spirited
chirrup of
a sparrow in
the rain.

grey
grey-black
blue-black
black

grey-black
white.

from **Tig**

[BLESSING THE ANIMALS]

then
    the spring-born population stays put
in its region of birth
    the Great Lakes of North America.

then
    of the autumn-born population
⅓ hibernates
    while the remaining ⅔
set out southwards
    on a narrow unwavering route.
it's a journey of 3000 kilometres
    down to south Texas/northern Mexico.

on arrival they gather in one or two
    valleys on particular conifers
in their millions
    & rest there till spring
& mate.

then this immense blizzard of wings
    begins to move northwards
travelling in a more leisurely way
    feeding & laying their eggs along the route ...

        the train's shadow
        flickering over the fields

the Monarch is a long-lived butterfly
    each individual surviving approximately
one year.
    their migration pattern is as follows

        a child nearby
        at a window

(migration pattern is as)

where the world
tracks past a

very young child
so happy so

taken aback
she

sings. (follows) & it beats
disclosing enclosing

flash! fold *flash!*
close slit show shock

blind shock black
shock/light exuding

over the visible
light intruding

on the visible
light corroding

the leaves leaving
only the light.

their

        dispersal   patterns

    are as   follows.

map.   stop.

count.   then

    immense   upsurge

      white   red

          amber   dark

the need for flattened bark-dwelling insects
to get away from predators on tree-trunks may
well have provided the selective pressure that
led to the evolution of wings—between rains
we lay listening lay waiting—you know me …

    rain on glass to the side of yr face

```
┌─────────────────────────────┐
│                             │
│                             │
│                             │
└─────────────────────────────┘
```

    a door shut in a corridor

[PICKING PERSIMMON]

distinctly through
the night air trains

through otherwise
silence—contact—

toy-like parallel
movements where machinery

clocks into place.
listen I saw what

I meant you saw
& the sunny external

world slid past over
yr shaded spectacles

& for the sake of
the rhythm I suppose

of the train on its
track you smiled.

it all takes you back.

under an intimate
intense cone of light

on a page on a desk
among books in the night

to return upturn upset
visit obsessive hating

obsessed teaching the
cocky ignorant well-to-do

offspring of the European
upper echelons to

limp along in something
like an intelligible

legible *béarlagair*
tax free on the button ...

I always liked being there
that dark & haunting house

off the South Circular
at the canal end where

colossal mirrors
spread out their

cloth ducks in flight
across a wall

oranges & lemons
& the bells

of St Clement's &
the strangeness

of flickering eyes
that are blind—

oh movements
continuous &

formal forgive
us our futures!

& loneliness.
& affection

that atom
incandescent

in the tune
the train's

shadow flickering
over the fields

mountains passing
(a city, distant)

gull-spots wheeling

a child nearby
at the window

where the world
tracks past a

very young child
so happy so

taken aback
she sings …

      & farre

                  exelle

         all other strowing

                    herbes

    for to decke up houses

                      slate

web

     clay

         weed

pebbles

     withered root

              dust

                        litter

  spider

     flicker of leaves lodged at the stub

    a tree

is a multiparticular planar miracle

is a book   an electronic blur   a minūte variation hook

is a door   a still   my notes   hats   quotes

the shadows moving in the breeze in the sunlight
beside the white house outside the village by the sea

change

---

found a nest
in a hedge

its centre a
weave of hair
from the family's
dog

silky oval precise
ly birdbody-size
no egg   some plastic
string.

[A PLACE TO STAY]

Go little thing   be good
black thread   spicule   white
solid radiant basis
carved cradled care-driven materials
twisting the texture
to him who has his senses still
baaah! goes the train on the line
yes & twisting she moves
& still—to balance—
arthritic & pert places in the spine
that plain stab-of-the-beak
& twist—*baaah!*—chance—a hand—
step—spread in the light—
see shade you don't dread
thread where you are a long
time-thing radiant
bright cone—*baaah!*—too—
not a word—
dough lolly loot
dough lolly loot.
good.

.

Profile to phonepiece
edged by light
a tenseness in the silence of the room
in the time it takes
catching a tangle of cables
the sun beyond the window
takes   it takes to &
the time it takes to

find out   is it
is it
really alright?

.

Nets in flight in the half-light
& has his senses still
& sense & has stillness
& sense
start up the stairs again
as early as you can

   there can be no very
to carry yr cares
   there can be no very
to pen the tune
   there can be no very
black melancholy
to him who
hurry
let's hurry across to the island
to see the notetaker
         soulmaker
         soulmate …

   woke   here is the
   nine o'clock   in the
   temperate zones   when
    I   you said to me

I see   (nine)   reading
my   quiet have I not
been   (news)   thinking
of you were there are

   some gaps here.

   Assembly of hounds

   Otherworldly sustenance

   Shelter of the wounded

   Power of the weak

   Dregs of clothing

   Most noble goodliness

CODA

a wisp of smoke from a village on a hilltop

a spider from a lamp

a bird saws   over & over   law-seem   daw-son   drop!

an apple   an egg

black points. gold stars. oily inside upper of a buttercup.

he just came in & sang some songs.

But what a price the Japanese women paid.

one such engraved amulet made of onyx presented to St Alban's Abbey by Aethelred the Unready

In the early days of broadcasting the BBC Advisory Committee on Spoken English helped those "whose daily duty it is to broadcast the world's news"

Scraping Bird   Bird-Twang   Squeak   Fiddle   flit from black to black

gaps   hollows   ridges   organized spaces

But what/this noise, what is it?

Did he say: it's yr mind   or it's *in* yr mind?

This is the first time I (see this film)

In medieval Denmark the custom of tying the skin of a white worm round the waist of the parturient woman prevailed.

to wake up

& resting ... to wake up, without echo, step by step, the green domes, gull on a flagpole, in the first place & stop ... but what/ this noise, what is it?

Echo says: you.

                        Then it's true?
                        Eyes get colder
                        & that changes

                        the luminous
                        instant/cut/
                        Bolder sd

                        Ominous

                        but does it? the sun
                        caught on rooftops
                        delays us

                        a silver dot
                        in the sky
                        making a bright white

                        line

                        too a noise
                        stormslapped flag
                        (& its absence:

> gull on a stone)
> pebbles that click on a wave's recession
> over a beach

> then ...

> So it's true?

Japanese women are not likely to bang a shoe on the table.

All that these able writers have said on language has been challenging, provocative, & generally very helpful.

Thank you.

                        clutching a bright
                                            blur of fruit
    your mother gave you
                                        you disappear into
            childhood   over a metal bridge
            & on to a train
                        for school forever.
                                            tact.
                the ceremony begins.
                                        black into white
                                                & back.
butterflies erupt & disappear over a hedge.
                                        seeds on a single gust
            across the neighbourhood
                                        you circle thus/quick
        where's my pencil?
                            is that a map?
                sails, distant.
                            cliffbase. flecks.
                    oily movements
                        in a pear-shaped stone.
                        burst of rain on the roof overhead.
                    that blunt instrument
                                    yr mind.
                        the ceremony begins
                            it all begins
                            all of it
                                all begins
                                over again
                                to
                                travel up to
                                let the eye travel
                                slowly
                                up the stem
                        green
                                up along it
                                in a pocket of light
                                leaves
                                    light cilia
                                    to the shaped
                                    silver in the air
                                    then
                                        to the flowers
                                    moving &
                    the leaves
                & the light in them
                                        up   inhale it
                                    pass   green blue red

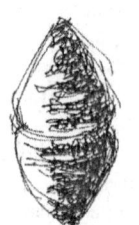

from **Humming**

SONNET SONG

Look: if the coin had landed on its edge making the
spaces to heads and tails the space of all probability
patterns lit up to date stretched to an evanescent blur
(one little thought experiment deserves another)
then *you* this, *me* that—*plink!*

                                            (knock)

If—rock of constancy, rubble of contingency—
(pass the salt) giving the bracket its due, its
space, its elastic content, bustle & itch
(where's my sandwich?) ah on the plate. *Pop!* It's gone.

                                            (knock)

If you dedicate your little book to Mammy and get
a prize—size matters—you know how it is—
a million years of isolation and neglect … as if you
deserve pampering *as by right.* Just write, right?

                                            (knock)

If a strange-looking fly walks across your page
in quick, short bursts, stops, grooms its back legs
thoroughly, you could say: with care, in this un-
believable world: look. At the evidence of literature,
the evidence of art and capital. The evidence of the
evidence.

                                         (knock-knock)

If the Way of Art is a Hard, Hard Way
as you heard some old Tin-Can say (dot)
loud sing cuckoo—grows seed—blows mead
and blossoms the wood now—

        If.

        If.

        If ...

Sing Cuckoo!

        [the letter *contend*
                the letter *ablaze*]

    If ...

    Put *that* on paper.
    Laugh. Emptily. Good grief.
    Is it?

                Knock

        Youbet.

        Thanks.

        Yep.

        OK.

        Right.

        Seeya.

Knock-knock

Ah yes, you're in an altered state.
But listen: so what? Who cares?
Where's my breakfast.
At 53: tickle me.
Food, fun, money, regularity.

Knock-knock

Knock-knock

Knock-knock

Now yr feet are on the ground. Now one foot,
now the other. The ground. The grass. Yr—
as yet undecorated—bones.
Over yr moving shadow—first this, then that—
little butterflies lift & flit—clocks circling—

> *what the heck—I wanted love—you*
> *wanted sex—tra-la cut the deck—*
> *yr fingers tremble—over what they—*
> *may resemble—in their future—(of*
> *bliss) tra-la—you know how it is*
> *tra-la—tick-tick but what the heck—*

who's there?

circles circling circuits. Circles circling—take
    yr pencil & make that call tick-tick
        there's work to do.

. .

Then a stray piece turned up called
THE DOG.

THE DOG

The dog is barking in the laneway again.
Who owns that dog? Do you?
Do you?

BALLAD

(Argument)

My brother is dead. I found him at the end of his bed.
His brain weighs 1565g, his heart 465
the document says & helps me know what a whiff
of actuality feels like from those who know the facts of life.

I am 52. How old are you? I'm old enough to take a knife
to any letter from the Arts Council for instance regretting et cetera
because they know I think by now—now that I'm older than
they are & longer on the job—I know perhaps a fact or two of life.

But wait! It's the middle of the night & time to wake up
I mean the middle of yr life & further along the ledge
past the diggers & set foundations parent birds attack.
You will discover starfish ingesting molluscs & ugly
dishonesties between people. You will have been a poet. Why?

What? At your age start again. From Scratch the dog to Doubt
the cat you stand (or hover) wondering if
you'll *ever* get to know the facts of life ...

I doubt it thought the cat, me too, the dog, & rattled off
a raga to the neighbouring territories. Grab that knife!
I know the facts are rough. Goodbye.

My brother is dead. His wristwatch laid face up beside his bed.

(Response)

   trees
hiss
   trees
bend
  &
sway
  &
grow
   that
way
  &
this
  the
trees
   whis-
per
   they …

…but
  do
you
  re-
  mem-
  ber
they
  tell
us
  can
you
  really
rem-
  ember

    depth
      colour
    mood
      mode
    fold
      &
    grip-
      code
    to
      never
    be
      still
    des-
      pite
    what
      you
    might
      think
    in
      all
    this
      space
    ever
      open
    to
      light
    up
      each
    twisted
      crease
            tickle of silk
            red tin bent
            plastic rusting
            wrought iron

```
              gritting a hinge
down derry derry
     light under a door
          who'd said a word
                knock
                          burn
&
  on
  the
    opp-
    osite
    bank
  there
    listen

listen
  in
  the
    dark
&
  in
  the
    dis-
    tance
    eyes
  pick
    out
  white
    flash-
  es
    that
  app-
    ear/
  dis-
```

    app-
ear
  where
rocks
  stop
one
  black
head-
  land
squat
  on
the
  sea.

-.-//Sing:
One flower—one stem—
sometimes a way in

catches an exit (of
power) but then one

flower (put the pen
down) (there) yes one

flower—one stem—
red shadow-pieces

that flicker I some-
times it's I was or

its exit opens on to
a yes/no twitch (pop

down will you & close it
up) each echoing chip

that multiplies what
little there is to

here: here: one stem—
two flowers—every

any other each this
way that a trace-patt-

ern that slips through
(follow it) one small

stone. One small stone.
Picked up. Looked at.

Put down. Pale dabs of
incense-dust that tap

paper on a windowledge—
XP352—while a bird's

.

song decides
　　　　/otherwise/
　　　　　　　　/otherwise//-.-

SONG

Take yr wristwatch off and lay it on the bed—
good—its three hands—*haa, ha-ha* & *ha-ha-ha*
—circling circumstance under heaven. (Move that
stone over there). I was carrying a little pain
in my head. There is every reason. Every reason.
Quickly getting the hang of a balanced eavesdrop
adventure, then moving on. Minutely. Receiving a
salary. Working hard, backwards. *Dear Upset.* Ways-
through difficult of access because of the/it's
because of the Clarity. Each millimetre bargained
for in the black/white grid between parent & child.
Then a sudden free space. Distorted places between
yr eye & the lens, yr eye & the surface, & yr eye
       & yr mindbits & the world. Or

ganized. Thursday. Once upon a time. Techno-savages
in the corridors waiting for image-hit and release.
Click. Crass. Wit and peeve. So. Oh look—there's
a landscape! A daisy closed over in overcast weather,
its pollen-stock, each tiny ricochet, safe and dry.
And something about bees ↗||↧ too and their recognition
////|| of colour. To see ultra-violet as a true colour↧↥↘
and to recognize the four distinct primal qualities
of the inner reticulate world: those which we call
jabber-of-magpie, gurgle-of-swallow, tricks-of-the-
robin-under-the-hedge.||||| I watched Rhetoric crawl
home one night and thought now there's a thing. All
the numerous hinges and springs, you know how it is—
no, no—of course you know ah-ha good. Right, so.
A seam, a stitch, a line of tiny zeros in the fabric
through which twists *this* to *this,* fluid thread, un-
dancing thread, appearing/disappearing, holding to-

gether what had not been, tight, fast, in place,
tacked in, a little way on. Drop by drop, grain by
grain ...

POEM

"This piece of paper you have just been handed is ...
Keep it. It advertises nothing, has no designs on you,
has come a long, long way, to here, in silence, in the
rain, free. As *you* are. You *are*. Now:
breathe ... "

from **Several Dances**

ON A LIGHT GROUND: EYE DANCE

Dapple of mother-spider
at the centre of its wet
web between a hedge & a
trellis. After work, the

wait. Place your foot
there. Then place it
there. Plonk a rock
in the pond: hear that

difference over there.
I-me-myself are moving
forward
            forward

to that left behind, through
air, to that placed shimmer
ahead. Forward. Carry your
spinning circle, a drop

lands, little by/connects
[pendent speck] reverberant.
Hold still. I do. Move. Stare.
Are you ready? What? To cross

which pattern a/pattern a/
[blank] ripple of leaf-shadow
over those books there
restless surges & retreats

smooth fluid undulations
that move across a vase
sketched in to burn care-
fully across representations

of small flowers on a curved
ceramic edge complications.
Pause. Meshes of energies
made visible. A calm [autumn]

morning in which pollen or
a calm autumn morning on
which a drift of rich [yellow]
pollen, a calm autumn morning

"outside [the community of] our
perceptions" in which outside
… which … I think (dab)

a fossil horizon, a dust horizon,
a mud horizon, the recent rising
of a nearby river, another fossil
horizon, one on top of the other

(small paint-marks on my palm,
wonder-swirl skin pattern, red
giant, white dwarf)—yes I

think I'll live here for a bit
not across no but along. One.
    Border. Forever.

ON A DARK GROUND: WORK DANCE

past a postage stamp stuck
sideways to the side of a
bookshelf going nowhere in
particular just now

past memory-flashes in tight dark
tangles open to the least access
of light stopped formally in code
in ink on paper in rows [blank]

wrapped up in stillness & expect-
ation &/past a weather here then
another there passing beyond past-
future (coil'd)((2, 3))(together)

weathers hitting the roof with a
red herring once in a blue moon
white as a sheet in a black mood
on a red letter day & so on a

jumble then two more (one ornate—
one spartan) take note coming all

the way down to treetops laughingly
referred to *as*. past that through
several nests one in particular I
remember *oh* down along an

uptilting branch through the
bark the feathers the downy warm
woven against the storm past
that sun catching green cloth

through glass here we go thorns
spindles twigs new & auton-
omous additions to the world
not representations of it

cackled an elderly stretcher
behind a canvas all dried up
scrap that sip yr tea Cranach
the Younger Scully the Unsub-

missive a tiny scalded insect
from a desk-lampshade for instance
to the page-top until *he was well-
loved* yr very breath disappears it

holding the falling world *he was
well-loved as an artist and as a
man* holding the falling world well.
who is that figure turning into

the doorway to go? a skull re-
members embers to re-invigorate
me-me-me-me-me/so. I'll deal you
plastic squares of the Absurd while

you shuffle the Possibilities-of-
the-Ridiculous over there, okay?

                done.

intent at desk in shed. relaxed
at table. reading in bed. working.
dreaming. breathing. drinking tea.
spearing fish spelling it out won-

dering wandering pondering
weaving a willow basket or two
on the damp riverbank billows of
mist over water at dawn. rules:

the ludicrous. the fragile. the
       indefensible.

give me some money. give me some
money to live. I'm willing to work.
I'm willing to work well. I'm willing
to work well and apply what talents

I have to the job. you will not get all
of me no but then I'll not get all of yr
money. give me some money. give
      me some money now.

LYRIC: BAL/ANCING

It's resolved.
This is what you need:
the wheels on the road
go *then—then—then.*

I draw the line
you do too
it's a blackbird
on a rooftip addressing

the neighbourhood
where all's in place
moving apart
& disappear-
ing leaving a trace.

How's yr hearing?
Pressed to the paper
ink wet softest at
the apical bud

       rend-

           ered into

alpha-

   bet out of

  the mouth

    &

   memory

         seed-

           pod

    burst & …

  & stones settle into
  their foundations
  in silence again.

  Watch them settle
  (no talking please)
  down here well.

MOUNTAIN RAILWAY: GAVOTTE

Drop a pebble in a pool: listen to it. Its
blue glistens. Black-gold-black. To glint,
tremble, stop. I turn off the radiator,
turn on the desk-lamp, sit, start. Here we
are. Soft pulses of light threading a small
hollow to contain the main phase in a fibrous
nest & the next move, the next move. One true
shimmering altercation. Then see. Oh all claim
that. Then don't. Let liars work. Enough is
enough as they say (vexed proof). Into their
    own dark trap. Drop a pebble in a pool.
                  Bow.

You plug the kettle in, hear it boil. Is
that the phone? Cup, spoon, milk. Good.
Do you really know then what you're about?
Say: work-shadow by screen-glow. Here is
the chorus that throws us more than (Who?)
we can ever predict. Crest on crest each
ripple moving out carries light into its
next receptive fold. Two crows fly low
following their shape exactly in the clear
sheen of the wet sand spread flat [tilt sur-
face to reduce glaze] underneath upside-
(beat for beat)-down. To land. Hello? Yes?
By the wave's edge. Holding a lit match, its
wavering apex, glint of sap below the heat-
line—each decisive moment, each precise
      flick—drop it in the dish & go.
                Now.

[HUNGARIAN] FOLK DANCE: ARTIST'S STUDIO

That job application
returned unopened
with a covering letter
thanking you for yr interest
and wishing you every
success in yr future
career Gaudate Deum
close window close it
tight (well) with finality
and panache you know
how it is in the Temple of
Echoes of Work Once Done
and return to the main case …

Symbol-evolving pattern-
obsessed idealistic creature
of cruelty and kindness in the
frustrating chaotic illogical
fantastic meaningless muck of
life you … stop and cede to
close window and return
to main page.

Strike a match, hold it steady,
things ignite the way you say
day goes into night, twist that
and scratch even if things are not
what they seem then close window
to return to main phase.

Look, mark it with yr pen,
the calendar says the 27th,
dot dot, a glint, in series,
in eternity, a tiny life—
look up—cold, heat, light—
that tendril following sun
through air rippled around a
stick thinking tra-la beyond thought …

    seems to read the blurred
    print on the back of the
    packet on the table amid
    the racket.

In reading something about
a "linguistic event" I spotted
a misprint and went to pencil
it in but pencilled the same
word a line below by mistake
(in which that word was *not*
a misprint) is that a linguistic
event or just a snippet from
a drifter's ballet? Bullet
snug in its chamber, quiet.

    Is blazoned on the back
    of the packet on the table.
    Stir the soup, tug the cable.

Did Goethe privilege a grand
bourgeois outlook and combine
it with an art which cosmetically
screens out the wrinkles of reality?
I wonder, shaving this morning,
moonlight a delight, but red
a warning.

Is streaming down the side
of the packet. A million
things happen at once. Can
you hack it? Dogs barking ...

Which brings us round again—
ladies step forward as the gents
fall back—to that job application
returned unopened this morning
thanking you for yr interest &
wishing you every success in yr
future career tra-la not so much
that you've just arrived but that
you'll never get there.

I look, you look, you look, I do.
Dance. A berry drops from a tree.
Here we are. Now. Put that in yr CV.
Engendering a systemic glytch in
the catalyst-catharsis matrix over
the Give/Receive pattern dynamic
so that it is impossible for us at
this moment in time to offer you a
dipped the brush-tip in then let fly
to receptive paper listening-thinking
impossible to offer you a offer you a
stamp those feet
& good.

TO BALANCE

       simper
    skit
      wad
  snag

Just the stitches in the fabric—*scuffle, snug, scrub, spatter, reef, snip, split, frolic*—particularly the stitches in the fabric, a bridge I know, a little house under it … what is that sound I'm hearing, a somehow *draped* structure around a core? The little beetle's upturned body in the sink. My hands waiting for something to happen …

    Do you like it?
    Yes, I do.
    Your shed
    your books
    your notebooks
    your time.

Most populations hardly notice the alphabets they live through, but when oral cultures come into contact with cultures that write, "literate" cultures—as we say—the oral culture, learning that alphabet, can move across its symmetries and strangenesses with a certain … sensitivity. So

    Cṁıoe é
      ᴅᴀṁe cnó
    ó c á n é
      p ó c á n ᴅ ó

is oral *and* lettrist—every word rhyming, every syllable rhyming, every *letter* finding its repetition (except the kiss, a plosive), a sort of spasm of self-conscious design (Celtic, bardic, academic even) from far away, in silence, and the Roman alphabet on goat's skin to the side of a Gospel, in Latin. There. Just the stitches in the fabric. But a girl's kiss too carrying across centuries in a handful of received letters. Nine of them in fact. Now, do the same in English.

RAIN DANCE

Payment was taken in advance. A calm autumn morning,
a long correspondence, a yellow dust. A small stone.
A way through. One swan, two goldcrests. Ants scamper-
ing along threads of sugary meaning. In the dappled
court far away one lived a regulated life. It has been

asserted that love is/love is lacking in this work (from
these works). Chance. Dot. The children have been dressed
and (they have been) each in (her) turn taken home.
Beautifully surprising light-tracking, light-hungry, light-
enticing plants on the forest floor. Tendril, panicle,

buttress. Travelling through their expertise, grim pingos,
treeless tundra (and that was the end of sweet Molly Mal-
who?) and getting (you did bring the sandwiches, yes?) really
a lot of (what?) nowhere fast (thanks), the God of Co-Co-Co-
Coherence in smithereens present and gaping at the terminus

wall changes everything. The man was taken back two days
after that. Dit-dot. What a moon! They did not talk (but)
only waited (there was no talking). They began (one began)
to speak of leading writers. Leading … *writers?* Dip. Dap.
    Tod. What on earth [my God] does that mean?

.

The first raindrop on the glass whose note is different to
the second and so the third—momentum, angle, mass—a
dance of—a fourth—and then a flicked spatter of several
more—a quiet dance for all that too, for you, here in the
dark, over yr head, comes together, speeds, spreads, then

slows—evenly—into a luminous quiet across each remembered
spot. It's not that Time(   )Flies, no, but that the past slipping back & elasticated can-will *ping!* forward into a possible future now/now any moment now any moment/moment (dash) duck! now. It is important that the public should not be given a

false picture. Plumes of steam across dark industrial
zones. Ear-tufts and ruffs, patterned wattles. Let's
have a cup of tea (said Polymath to Polyglot). Let's
certainly. Good, yes, thanks a lot. High pressure, low
cloud, where do we go from here? Close the windows,

lock the house, it'll all be fine in the end, my dear.

> looked up dodging dogshit gladdened no
> matter sirens this must be
> Nature

> though not my nature or yours for that/
> three to five pm/am
> could be

> twelve noon—who cares—look up—
> here we go under-
> ground

> touching the inner corners of the category
> then wince back
> shocked.

> learning takes a turn. butterflies pass.
> busy picturing the
> fabric of

the sky—peaks—hollows—whirlpools—how
wind in trees—& trees
in air—

of air at speed against birds that
wheel
&

pivot over the bay—there's ground enough to
go around/twice. &
twice again.

a crease on page. shadow. light.

When you were a little boy, then a little man, then
a big, bursting, raging young man, then calmer, calmer,
finally older and to the point and you could say, yes:
some small distinct shadows across an envelope on a desk
before posting, or, falling from the sky, one snowflake,
detached, its patterns of descent, its dance, with a
million others, and the wind—dashes, floats, twists,
slips, hovers—a little boy again. When payment is
taken in advance …

LOCKET

Place yr cup

on the table

look up

what's that?

NEIGHBOURING DOORS (CEREMONIAL DANCE)

    two tape recorders
                  one glasses-case
  one desk-lamp
                two staplers
  one mug
                several pens
  one pencil
                one pencil holder
  two pencils
                four erasers
  three sharpeners
                a pinecone
  two incense sticks
                & a
  small
                bottle of

homeopathic medicine.

.

plastic pen holder
                several pens
a red pencil stub
                a black tyre-valve cap
an acorn
                my father's
greenish-blue pen
                inscribed

to SJ Scully from all at Spicers

      Aug 1955

.

    bottle of Tipp-Ex
            tower of books
    to my right
            tower of books
    to my left
            tower of books
    & notebooks

        opposite.

•

    one soapstone dish
            one walnut
    one acorn
            one acorn cup
    one

        dried lime leaf
            with pods.

•

    two bottles of vitamins
            one small calendar
    two incense sticks
            four erasers
    three pencil sharpeners
            nine postcards.

        dance.

•

    one copybook
             one hardback notebook (blue)
    a wooden bowl
             with papers
    a small framed
             (geometric) pastel drawing
    a storage box
             with incense sticks and papers

        sundry papers

          postcards

           dust.

.

        expectation.

          enough.

          . .

(Dapple

from **Work**

GEOMETRIC
[for gamelan]

I hadn't realized that
that bird-phrase from
that magpie is quite
that of a laying hen's
too till now as languages
overlap & slap together
making a music you're
making a music you're
too busy trying to catch
to really notice that house
you passed last night by
chance for instance you
part grew up in where cars
pass, pass. Odd & solid.

.

There's the past.
Here's the future.
A to B. Connect.
Watch this ball.
A to B to B
to A. Slap. Tear.
When a dandelion's
picked it pops: its
hollow stalk, its
white sap, its
stark ring, its
little laugh. There
is so much bird-

song in this pocket
of presence too we
recommend you stop
now & listen to
the bough-top. Good.
To the Blackbird of
Triangulation, Cats
& Scribal Memory.
Before moving on.

. .

Where the page
curves in to its
binding & light
pours down from
an overhead lamp
like that (like this)
eyes meet surface
stitch with stitch
text to one side
image to the other
& laugh.
Sparks.
Print.
And start again.

. . .

From this beach here you can watch a cargo ship
come in to port, a jet tilt turning to land, a sky
lark rising in its translucent tube of what could
be its flight to vantage & descent along that rippled
territorial abstract that descends gently here to you

            lost among
            steel plates
        ropes pullies winches
          welding cradles
            at a bench
          in a workshop
          in the shadows
        at the back of the
      Black Glowering Factory
      I mean Foundry of the
              well
             the ....
          Imagination.
           Toodle-oo.

         Wind sand waves
           hiss as they
          make contact
            with what
             someone
          at some stage
        somehow got to call
            solidity
           (some joke)
         & break & start
           to slide past
          that last mark
           yr feet made
          on the ground
              again.
         A quarter past
               two.
         What's it to you?

      Falling together
    (fissure, monument)
      and gathered
        in one.
    Before moving on.
        Good.

      . . . .

writing a little poem for
someone directly in
that way something
I almost never do
but in this dream
working content
into the shade out of
the heat with a light
stick in the sand until
a detail in the distance

fats & thins where a bird
on a far wall clears
(the impossible poetry
of the closed heart chakra)
comes, goes, watching
that slight movement
in the shade in the morning
in hunger (flower-edges
flare back) so much so
much in whiteness gone

it was rough notes
smooth ideas & a

willowy chorus
brought us thus far
dear writing something
for someone directly in
the shade under the
moving trees there
in an outburst of
description & the absurd
over a flat watercolour
on some plaster priming
on gauze mounted
on cardboard.

. . . . .

Is that enough? A little-dog bark, two tones, incessant, with regular 5/10 intervals: *off-off. Off-off. Off-off.*

.

Clubbed antennae, coiled proboscis—that's him!

.

A memo is not an omen.

.

I always thought. Until we got stuck in the airport.

.

"255 Material" is written on a box on a top shelf.
"Super Valu—values you!" is printed on a box
beside it. Not content with nocturnal flights of
the imagination in yr tent I can't really see what
you meant. Well.

.

An omen fits its moment. Neatly. At least.

.

So dark the morning it could be almost night.
That time of year here when it's hard to tell.
But tell me.

.

Memorable omissions, no mention of aim,
mean tones, amen. Label that.

.

Your eyes meet the world in the morning: a box on a
shelf, some books, birds, day-sound of light rain
on a roof, trees moving, distant traffic. Beg a
question, get an answer. Goddess of Worry, release
me, Devil of the Arrow of Time—let fly! Parallels,
diagonals, circles & bent squares, where are we?
Devils of Dimension, disimprison me. Flick through
yr experiential Repertoire, see what happens; listen;
forget. Get up! I did. You saw. We played. At last.
Is that enough?

SETTING
[for guitar]

Back that into a corner.
Park it over there. Let's
go to the park & take a
walk under its trees, leading
lines in steps together that
go back, back far (park that
car, let's go) branched &
growing still, moving, clicking
a little in this winter morning
breeze. Tap. Take care.

  Well, that's past.
  I taught that
  lesson & it's past.
  I drove past

  trees—not fast
  the traffic was
  terrible—& got
  there late at

  last. Of course.
  The special
  pleasure of step-
  ping over park-

  land peppered
  with last year's
  hardened beech
  mast or (you're

  an artist, yes?)
  the elasticity of
  time sluicing past
  its cast iron image

    of itself twisting
    in its flask to rip
    it & its brief
    occupants apart

    is worthy of note.
    Take heart. Don't
    fret. People are
    wonderful. But

    do they last? Let's
    take that walk

we talked about now (are you awake?)
along this black/blank path, each footstep
on the map, block, each arm-swing, each
eye-face contact with what's outside,
connected in that bright dark pool (quick
strum) which I (we) think is inside you
for sure you call (block) what, yes, each
unplanned pebble-knock, each bird-dot
going by in opening twilight (it's dawn)
each whispered connection I know you
know about following & enwinding.
Good to be alive. A little longer. Along
the world-sheet. Out-&-about. To watch
our children. To imagine the next chord.

This must be an Affected Place. And this
must be another Affected Place; sharp
arrow arriving and pointing down. Where
the arrow lands, bury me. Placed. I
remember (I was very young indeed) perched
on my father's knee, he reading Robin Hood
to me in the garden by that purple shrub.
Life's arrow. Life's Affected Places. Dodge
this arrow now—quick flick—divert from
that Place sharply. And remember: Design
for a Cloak, Underwater Pyramids, Light-
    Broadening, Illuminated Leaf.

LONG BLOCK

when
    plate
meets
    plate
& stamps
    in place
a piece
    to
firm
    it
fair &
    square
a sort
    of
vertical
    instant
climbing
    printing
skywards
    up
    [That's what's good about it. What?
    Its date. The 5th of the 4th zero 8?
    And the very early morning sun &
    the quiet. And the breeze, its sound
    in the leaves outside. Clack of magpie.
    Whisper of the pen on the page.]
listen
    take it

down
    how many
dark
    patches
how much
    little
writing
    little
hand-
    writing
how many
    little
impact
    bits
there
    now?

pluck a
    dandelion:
its stem
    pops –
oozes:
    one white
o. but
    what's
the bloody
    use if
you can't
    make
peace
    go out
meet people
    eat

  drink
    laugh
     gabble
      gabble
       gabble
     as the
    Gabble
   Plant
   grows
around
   its
pergola
  gossip-
blossoms
   vicious-
  petalled
   strange-
scented?
  here
we are
  alive
& looking.
  & the
fruit?
  ah let's
see yes
  those
tough bright
  balls of
pressed
  pellets

of poison
    might be
quite delicious
    too at
the outset
    but …

woven
    through
a water-
    spout
from a
    stone fish's
mouth
    light
hits the
    back of
the
    fountain—
the mind—
    in this
village
    near the
mountains
    & the
strong reg-
    ular song
of water
    hitting
water in
    the bottom
of a trough
    just
        laughs

        laughs
           laughs.

they fall
   together
the small
   words
gathered
   in a quiet
corner
   glad to
find them
   or happy
to know
   that when
you think
   to look
drop-
   lets of
connect-
   ive
gel you
   take in
as a
   child
& use
   until you
die &
   they die
with you
   this per-
sonal orn-
   ament-
ation these

     quietly
unique
     idiosyncrasies—
minute
   unrecorded
       disappearing—
keep
   their place
in the
   fluidly
mapped
   geometry
of the
   improvised:
or.
   this.
      now.
one strange
   Tuesday in
winter one
   extra-
ordinary
   Otherday in
spring. sharp-
   coloured
pebbles in
   yr pocket
yr workshop
   yr pens &
pencils
   the work
done
   continuing
among the

        unforgotten
    the un-
        forgettable.
  now ...

  all this.

We covered the surface of
each gravure plate with litho
ink producing mirror images
in negative so we placed them
in order side by side from
left to right to get it right.

Good.

NOTES

Things That Happen [1981—2006], a work in eight books & three chapbooks, is currently available as a four-volume set: *5 Freedoms of Movement, Livelihood, Sonata* & *Tig.* The chapbooks, *Prelude, Interlude* & *Postlude,* may still be available separately from Wild Honey Press. Like all Wild Honey Press poetry chapbooks they are beautifully done, worth searching out.

The dates for *Things That Happen* represent the period of composition. The dates to individual books are the dates of publication. I have been writing & publishing since the early '70s, but have included nothing from that decade here. Several further years' work from the *Things That Happen* project have not been represented either because of the difficulty of coherent excerption.

Things That Happen in its entirety is written around motifs and sub-motifs. The motifs interlace in waves and eddies which echo and deepen as the reader progresses. The project is structured radially so that you can dip in almost anywhere and pick up the music of the interlacing motifs. This is the driving pulse of the work. The main difference for the reader, I suppose, is the opportunity to enjoy the relationships between pieces as well as the pieces for themselves and, crucially, to shift the usual balance of emphasis a little so that it becomes clear this field of relation is the formal matrix of the work itself. My hope is this sampler will send some readers back to the originals.

Three new books, *Humming, Work* & *Several Dances,* built around their own separate motifs, are due from Shearsman Books [UK], Oystercatcher Press [UK] and Ahadada Books [Japan] respectively, in 2009.

My sincerest thanks to Dedalus Press for making this book available in Ireland.

A few words on the Irish language snippets:

P 32: *Do-chum glóire Dé agus onóra na hÉireann:* for the glory of God & the honour of Ireland [motto of the old Irish Press newspaper].

p. 33: *do ghlam nach binn:* yr ugly roaring, from Aogán Ó Rathaille's magnificent *Is fada liom oíche fhírfhliuch gan suan, gan srann.* The poet is addressing the sea, upon which he vainly hopes for help from Spain.

nóinín: daisy
neantóg: nettle
bainne bó bleacht: cowslip
feochadán: thistle
sabhaircín: primrose
fraoch: heather

fite fuaite: tightly interwoven
An tosach, ar deireadh: The beginning, finally.

p. 36: *Gósta garbh-Bhéarla:* a smattering of uncouth English

p. 63: *clé deas:* left right, or—punningly—"a fine piece of work by Paul Klee".
It might be worth noting here re FIRE pp 61—65 that the term "aa" (say "a" as in "face") in Sesotho means "yes".

p. 83: *Oifig an Phoist:* Post Office. The "impossible accent" is a *fada* or acute accent on the "p".

Éist, éist liom: Listen, listen to me.

p. 125: *Tig:* house. English sense intended also. The titles in square brackets (pp 127 - 135) are those of naive paintings.

p. 131: *béarlagair:* jargon

p. 137: Closing 6 lines are translations of some *briatharogham,* cryptic 2-word glosses on ogham letter-names found in medieval mss (though thought to be much older than this). Meant to be mnemonic.

p. 172: *Cride é*   he is my heart
      daire cnó   nut of the oak
    ócán é   he is a young man
      pócán dó   a kiss for him

•

Finally, the marks in the second stanza of 'Song' on p 156 are not misprints.

www.ingramcontent.com/pod-product-compliance
Lightning Source LLC
Chambersburg PA
CBHW032253150426
43195CB00008BA/438